POSITIVE PASSAGE

EVERYDAY KWANZAA POEMS

▼

by JohnnieRenee Nia Nelson

Cover Design by Judythe Sieck

Copyright © 1992 by
JohnnieRenee Nia Nelson.
All rights reserved.
Published by
House of Nia
4014 Calmoor Street
National City, CA 91950
U.S.A.

**POSITIVE PASSAGE: EVERYDAY
KWANZAA POEMS** was developed
in part by a grant from the National
Endowment of the Arts Emerging
Arts Fund of the San Diego Community
Foundation.

<u>NGUZO SABA</u>

- **UMOJA (Unity)**

- **KUJICHAGULIA (Self-determination)**

- **UJIMA (Collected Work and**

    Responsibility)

- **UJAMAA (Co-operative Economics)**

- **NIA (Purpose)**

- **KUUMBA (Creativity)**

- **IMANI (Faith)**

To the "BENZ" in my life

BENNIE

BENNETT

&

**Brandon
Emil
Nelson**

JOURNEY

ANCESTRY

AMINATA'S SONG

BLACK GOLD

SHONA

MASAI MEN

ROUND TRIP HOME

ODYSSEY

FAMILY TREE

FROM THE MOTHERLAND

DRUM CALL

UMOJA

WHAT YOU DO

KWANZAA CONSCIOUSNESS

NIA II

GOING THE DISTANCE

NGUZO SABA INFERENCES

ACROPHOBIA

IMANI ANTHEM

IMANI ALWAYS

THE RICHES OF KWANZAA

KUUMBA

CHILD SONGS

LULLABIES

I AM RIVER

LEGACY

KARENGA

WHY KWANZAA WAS CREATED

KWANZAA QUILT

ZAWADI

SPIRITUAL RITUALS

KENTE CLOTH KWANZAA

ANCESTRY

AMINATA'S SONG

When you see me styling
Wrapped in my kinetic/kemetic kente
You're witnessing one of many "gente"
Expressing in me.

I've got some people in me
I've got some people in me
Look closely and you will see
I am Ashanti
A am Fulani
I am Kanuri
I am Kwangali
I am Lozi
I am Mbuti
I am Swazi
I am Tutsi
I am Twi.

See the Ngai
See the Ouadai
See the Masai
See the Songhai

<u>AMINATA'S SONG</u> (Continued)

See the Vai
Expressing in me.

I can sing in tongues galore,
Shona, Bemba Swahili, Hausa,
And many, many more
Kwanyama, Yoruba, Xhosa and Kru
Mandika, and Walamo - just to name a few
I am an international polyglot
Because of all the people I've got
Expressing in me
I've got some people in me
I've got some people in me

Look closely and you will view
The me that is Zulu
The me that is Tubu
The me that is Sotho
The me that is Nkundu
The me that is Sala Mpasu
The me that is Kikuyu
The me that is Hutu

AMINATA'S SONG (Continued)

The me that is Embu
The me that is Budu.

Look at me and you will see
More than a diasporan entity
Who is Panamanian
Who is Jamaican
Who is Haitian
Who is Puerto Rican
Who is Bahamian
But rather a Pan African entity
From my Liberian eyes
To my Tanzanian thighs
From my Ghanian lips
To my Somalian hips
From my Gambian face
To my Egyptian waist
From my Zimbabwean toes
To my Nigerian nose
And my Ibo elbows.

I've got some people in me
I've got some people in me
AMINATA'S SONG (Continued)

<u>AMINATA'S SONG</u> (Continued)

Who manifest in all that I do
In my thoughts and my point of view
In my hair and in my clothes
In my poetry and my prose
In my demeanor and my style
In my laughter and my smile
In my walk with my heavy head load
In my manner and my fashion mode
And most especially in my genetic code
And yours!!!

BLACK GOLD

Often when I was little
Big Mama would tuck me in my bed
And read to me the most beautiful story
Anyone had ever read.
She'd wait 'til I was still and quiet
Before she'd even start
And as the words flowed from her mouth
They touched upon my heart.
The story that she would tell me was
The "Greatest Story Ever Told"
About the world's most valuable natural
resource
-authentic black gold.
"Black gold is not a metal
Nor an oil known as petroleum
It's the essence of an African people
-People you descended from
It's our history and our traditions
It's our cultural celebrations

BLACK GOLD (Continued)

It's the sum total of our achievements
Which gave rise to such great nations
As Ghana, Egypt, Songhai and Mali
Great empires of antiquity
Black gold originated in Africa
The birthplace of humanity"
And as I drifted into dreamland
She'd whisper from afar
"Black gold is your ancestral legacy
The quintessence of who you are."

As far back as I can recall
I remember being told
Wondrous tales of my African heritage
And of my people - pure black gold.

SHONA

Among the Shona
A family's success
Is weighed by their children's happiness
And the family's state of health
Not by the accumulation of material wealth
Shona people sure are wise
To have the foresight to emphasize
Values that strengthen family ties
Traditions of sharing,traditions of caring
Traditions that instill dignity and pride
That generate beauty on the inside.
Among the Shona
The joy children bring
To the family union
Is the most valued thing
Along with the laughter that families share
And a respect and an appreciation for others
Found everywhere.
Shona people sure are wise
To have the foresight to emphasize
Values that strengthen family ties
Traditions of sharing, traditions of caring
Traditions that instill dignity and pride
That generate beauty on the inside.
That generate beauty on the inside.

MASAI MEN

I find it peculiar how every now and then
My mind gets to thinking on Masai men
Reknowned for their courage
And their magnificient physiques
They occupy my thoughts for weeks upon weeks.
These men who walk with their heads held high
Whose very demeanor seems to imply
A high self esteem and a strong sense of worth
The most dignified and distinguished men on earth.
These sage traditionalists with cattle-breeding expertise
And long thick hair groomed with red clay and cow grease
I find intriguing; fascinating;
Enchanting, alluring, captivating .
And when they do that leap dance that they so expertly do
I find myself wishing that I also knew
How to make my body jump four stories high
To face a giraffe
Eye to eye.

ROUND TRIP HOME

When you return to Africa for the first time
you're greeted by "Jambo" and "Hello"
and rhetorical questions:
"Are you Negroes?"
"No Swahili?"
"Why have you been so long coming home"?
You're treated to national dishes such as Nshima
and fleshy coconuts alien to diasporan Africans
You're entertained by ephemeral orange islands
created by sunsets
And Makishi dances honoring African womanhood
with supple sensuality
You're wooed by a philosophy of humanism
so endemic to your soul
you won't need to take a "101" anything
to understand its assumptions or
comprehend its tenets.
When you return to Africa for the first time
you won't need a round-trip ticket to get home.

ODYSSEY

FAMILY TREE

My roots are a mystery
Dark branchings of an unidentified tree
And I'm a disconnected, transplanted entity
In search of my family's unearthed identity
Which tree is my family tree?
Is it the baobab massive and mighty
Revered for its versatility; Could that be
the progenitor of my genealogy?
Is it the Mangrove tree
standing on stiltlike roots
Or does my family tree bear nuts and fruits?
Is it the banyan tree with its roots in the air
This one tree forest; Is that from where
My African lineage began
In the air as opposed to the land?

Is my family tree a sacred tree
Believed to hold healing powers
Or is it an acacia tree
Famed for its fragrant flowers?
Did my family tree originate in Mali
Or Chad or Liberia or Ghana

FAMILY TREE (continued)

Or did it originate in Togo or Benin,
Nigeria or Botswana?
Are there leaf scars on my family tree
Where stems were snatched
From their branches
And dispersed throughout the universe
By European avalanches?
Is my family tree a special
Imbued with special features?
Is it an iroko prized by sculptors
Or a haven for anguished creatures ?

So many trees indigenous to the forestry
From where my ancestors came!
Red ironwood, ebony, African mahogany
Mopani, starpelia and flame!
With all of these questions going unanswered
I suspect that my family tree
Will forever remain an enigma
A Kano knot mystery.

FROM THE MOTHERLAND
TO THE MAYALAND

From the Motherland to the Mayaland
We came before Columbus
And where the pyramids pierce the skies
Is where our architecture belies
Their efforts to keep the truth from us

The Africans and the Aztecs
Both architects of cultural links
Created monuments now as mysterious
As the riddle of the Sphinx
There are few places in the world
Where pyramids can be found
Where gua-nin from African spears
Lay buried in the ground

We were a seafaring people
Who knew that the earth wasn't flat
Who had advanced science and technology
And based upon that

FROM THE MOTHERLAND
TO THE MAYALAND

Came to the shores of this hemisphere many times
In our own vessels; in our own ships
We came as traders not as conquerors
With maps created by African minds
and drawn by African fingertips

From the Motherland to the Mayaland
We came before Columbus
And lest we lose our truth
We must teach our youth
The truth that they for so long kept from us
That we came 3,000+ years before Columbus.

DRUM CALL

From drum call
To curtain call
We celebrate the Kwanzaa spirit
From dawn to dusk
You will find us
Ever ready to revere it.

For seven days
In many ways
We celebrate our roots
And when we're through
Here's what we do
We enjoy our Kwanzaa fruits.

<u>UMOJA</u>

They all come when they hear the drums
The Uncle Bens and Uncle Toms
The militants and the oreos too
Line up to form the Kwanzaa queue.
They all come to be blessed
With a Kwanzaa consciousness
They all come for their yearly dose
Though traumatized and comatose.
The luminaries and the visionaries
Come hand and hand with their snowberries
The culture vultures when they hear the beat
Get there first to grab a front row seat
They come out of the woodwork;
They come out of thin air
They come out of the closet:
They come out of nowhere
They come running, they come panting
When they hear the drumming
When they hear the chanting
They come. They all come. And they are welcome.

WHAT WE DO

What we do says who we are

Falling rock or rising star

What we do, not what we preach

Is the lesson that we teach

is the message that we send

-Not what we intend.

Our everyday activity

States loud and clear who we be.

KWANZAA CONSCIOUSNESS

The source of my happiness
Is my Kwanzaa consciousness
I celebrate Kwanzaa all year long
In daily deed; in thought; in song
Each day I sing a song of praise
For the progress I've made in learning new ways
Of incorporating the values of this noble event
Into my daily routine; Everyday is spent
Engaging in activities which yield spiritual fruits
Activities which reflect my African roots
I know that I've been truly blessed
To have a Kwanzaa consciousness.

NIA II

Hold your dream in high esteem

Show respect for the goals you set

Feel compelled to excel

Have a mission not just ambition

Keep the faith, hang in there, and commit.

Make purpose and dedication

Your daily aspiration

Give praise for your successes always

Revere that which is dear

Celebrate that which is great

- Yourself and your Kwanzaa holidays

GOING THE DISTANCE

Going the distance
No matter how far
If you're truly determined to be successful
You already are.

Going the distance
Means moving your feet
And persevering during times
When you'd rather retreat.

Going the distance
Means being focused and fit
Means acknowledging and affirming
Your ability to commit.

<u>GOING THE DISTANCE</u> (Continued)

Going the distance
Means chasing your dream
Means doing the things necessary
To nurture your self esteem.
Replacing fear with faith
Gives you the strength
To go the distance
To go the length

Going the distance
No matter how far
If you're truly determined to be successful
You already are.

NGUZO SABA INFERENCES

Don't expect to promote unity
If you're planning on working alone
Don't expect to express creativity
If you're content to be a clone
Don't expect things to happen
Without taking the initiative
Don't expect to lead a purposeful life
Without learning how to give
Don't expect a sense of direction
To come from without
Don't expect faith to reign
If you're demonstrating doubt.
Don't expect to ever be
All that you can be
If you're unwilling to adopt a
Kawaida philosophy.

ACROPHOBIA

"Never fear heights," my mother admonished
"If you want to receive your just reward
For acrophobia is a luxury
Children of color can ill afford
How are you going to climb
The ladder of success
When a fear of heights
Leaves you powerless?
How are you going to reach your highest peak
When the thought of elevation leaves you
cringing and weak?
How are you going to rise
To the top
When you're immobilized
By the possibility of a drop?
With a fear of heights you can never entertain
Lofty ambitions or hope to reign

ACROPHOBIA (Continued)

Among the distinguished, the exalted
Among the eminent
Acrophobia will prohibit your ascent."

"A fear of heights
Will not allow you to soar
Will not allow you to tower
And furthermore
It's a vicious dreamkiller
That will not allow you to scale
The walls of opportunity
It will cause you to fail."
"So, never fear heights," mother again advised
"If you 're to have your high hopes realized."

IMANI ANTHEM

My faith is my fortune
Active faith enriches me
My everyday activities demonstrate
The faith I need to be
And the universe acknowledges my efforts
And rewards me generously
And allows me to experience
Unlimited prosperity.

My faith is my fortress
Spiritual rituals strengthen me
Affirmations and meditation
Enable me to live triumphantly.
My faith is as rooted as
An ancient baobab tree
My faith has the power to diminish
Fear, doubt and adversity.

IMANI ANTHEM (Continued)

My faith is my future
The key to my destiny
By faith I know what I envision
Will soon be my reality .
My faith can work wonders
When it is energized
My faith _is_ my future
Today's hopes actualized.

IMANI ALWAYS

Open your eyes
For the sun will rise
And the dawn will spawn
Faith anew.
The fear that is here
Will soon disappear
As a spark in the dark
Turns into
A promise fulfilled
A new day revealed
Hope emerging gloriously.
So open your eyes
Face the dark skies
Then see your sun/self rise
Victoriously.

THE RICHES OF KWANZAA

The riches of Kwanzaa
Are not found in the zawadi
But in the everyday Kwanzaa canons
We embody.

KUUMBA

The basis of all our creations is
Gumbo ya ya
It can be found in all African nations
This gumbo ya ya
It's in our fashions and our quilting
It's integral to the Maishi dancer's stilting
It's in our tapping
in our rapping
In our music
yeah all that jazz
In everything our culture has.
Gumbo ya ya/ Allows for multiple voice
Gumbo ya ya/Allows for personal choice
Gumbo ya ya/Allows for individuality
Gumbo ya ya
The basis of African creativity.

Gumbo ya ya
Polyrhythmic improvisations
Gumbo ya ya
Individualistic variations
Leads us to one destination.

CHILD SONGS

I

Our children are our STAR pupils
And we as their parents
and their first teachers
Must teach our rising STARS
About the beauty of their
 midnight features.

II

Our children are:
Black pearls
African violets
Black gold
Midnight suns
Hope diamonds
Black magic.

LULLABIES

I

Hush little baby and don't you cry

Big Mama's gonna hum a blues lullabye

And if you wil but listen, you'll hear your reward

In Etta James' and Bessie Smith's jazzy blues chord.

II

Hush diasporan baby and don't you weep

Steel band music will lull you to sleep

Direct from Trinidad, creative gifts abound

Pan music for Pan-African ears, listen to the sound.

LULLABIES (Continued)

III

Hush Pan-African baby and don't you cry
Mother Africa is singing her Limpopo lullabye
And if you will but hush for just a little while
You will be nursed by the Nile.

IV

It's nationtime and the living is easy
Along the Nile, along the Zambesi
But in South Africa the living is not
So wail on little baby we understand your lot.

I AM RIVER

I am river forever flowing
forever knowing
an unlimited energy source
I am Niger, Zambezi,Congo,
Kalahari, Orange. Limpopo,
and Nile
Mile upon mile
of indomitable force

I am lake forever still
forever tranquil
irrevocably serene and calm
I am Nyasa,Tanganyika,
Turkana, Volta, Kariba
and Chad
A chiliad
of placid psalm

I am river, I am sea
paradoxical duality

≈≈≈≈≈≈≈≈≈≈≈

LEGACY

<u>KARENGA</u>

A man of vision

Once made a decision

That he wouldn't wait

For others to legislate

A special day of celebration

For diasporan Africans in this nation

So he in the spirit of creativity

Created Kwanzaa /Afrocentricity

At its best.

The rest

Is history.

WHY KWANZAA WAS CREATED

First, Kwanzaa was created to reaffirm and restore
Our African heritage and our African culture
Secondly, Kwanzaa was created to introduce
and reinforce the "Nguzo Saba"
Umoja, Kujichagulia, Ujima, Ujamaa, Nia,
Imani and Kuumba;
Thirdly, Kwanzaa was created to address
the absence of non-heroic holidays in the
national African American community
To cultivate communal rituals around major
events and issues in communal history and culture
(thereby promoting unity)
Fourthly, Kwanzaa was created to serve
as a regular communal celebration
Which reaffirms and reinforces the bonds between us
as a people; as a nation.
And fifthly, Kwanzaa was created as an act
Of cultural self-determination
As a self-conscious statement of our cultural truth
As a beginning towards its revitalization

As written by Maulana Karenga
These are the reasons why Kwanzaa was created
Honorable reasons, ambitious reasons,
That didn't need to be debated.

THE KWANZAA QUILT

My security blanket
Was a Kwanzaa quilt
A unique creation
Big Mama built
From fabric and batting
With needle and thread
A zillion stitches
Of black, green and red

It was a cloth of honor
I displayed with much pride
It was a cultural document
With coziness and warmth inside
Big Mama made that kwanzaa quilt
especially for me
In the spirit of kuumba (creativity)
To pay tribute to our family
To pay tribute to Kwanzaa
To honor our African ancestry.

ZAWADI

Gifts of time and effort
I give daily to my children
Accompanied by praise
I read to them
I listen to them
I tell them in many ways
How very much I love them
And how much it means to me
To have them in my life
As part of my reality.

Gifts of joy and laughter
My children daily bring to me
And I accept eagerly
Their zawadi.

SPIRITUAL RITUALS

The pouring of libation on special occasions
In the direction of the four winds
I do in remembrance of my ancestors
When I gather among family and friends.
To connect with my African roots
I engage in activities which yield spiritual fruits.

The lighting of candles during Kwanzaa week
Is a spiritual ritual I annually employ
I practice traditions which honor my heritage
Traditions that I enjoy.
To connect with my African roots
I engage in activities which yield spiritual fruits.

KENTE CLOTH KWANZAA

I wish for you a Kente cloth Kwanzaa
Royal, rhythmic and resplendent
Wondrously woven with golden threads
And silken symbols
From ancestral rituals
Distinctive and vibrant
Steeped in meaningful tradition
Aesthetic, artistic and esoteric
An encoded keepsake; a weave
To wrap up fond memories
To dress up diasporan dreams
To cocoon your soul.

JohnnieRenee Nia Nelson is a native Chicagoan currently residing in California. She is a member of the African American Writers' and Artists' Guild of San Diego and has been involved with numerous programs in the area. Her first volume of poetry "21 Years Toward Becoming a Black Woman" received the MSU Creative Writing Award for Best Collection of Poetry. In 1988 Ms. Nelson wrote A Quest for Kwanzaa which has been heralded as the authoratative genesis of Kwanzaa literature. Ms. Nelson has traveled extensively throughout Africa, Europe, Canada and the Caribbean and is currently completing two works in progress, THE KWANZAA CANONS and BLACK BEAUTY: POEMS ABOUT OUR PEOPLE.